A TRUE BOOK™

The California Gold Rush

MEL FRIEDMAN

Children's Press®
An Imprint of Scholastic Inc.
New York   Toronto   London   Auckland   Sydney
Mexico City   New Delhi   Hong Kong
Danbury, Connecticut

Content Consultant
David R. Smith, Ph.D.
Adjunct Assistant Professor of History
University of Michigan
Ann Arbor, Michigan

Library of Congress Cataloging-in-Publication Data

Friedman, Mel, 1946–
  The California Gold Rush / by Mel Friedman.
       p. cm.—(A true book)
  Includes bibliographical references and index.
  ISBN-13: 978-0-531-20581-5 (lib. bdg.)   978-0-531-21244-8 (pbk.)
  ISBN-10: 0-531-20581-9 (lib. bdg.)   0-531-21244-0 (pbk.)

1. California—Gold discoveries—Juvenile literature. 2.
California—History—1846-1850—Juvenile literature. I. Title. II.
Series.

  F865.F83 2010
  979.4'04—dc22   2009017524

All rights reserved. Published in 2010 by Children's Press, an imprint of Scholastic Inc.
Published simultaneously in Canada. Printed in China.
SCHOLASTIC, CHILDREN'S PRESS, A TRUE BOOK, and associated logos are trademarks and/or registered trademarks of Scholastic Inc.

1 2 3 4 5 6 7 8 9 10 R 19 18 17 16 15 14 13 12 11 10   62

Find the Truth!

Everything you are about to read is true *except* for one of the sentences on this page.

Which one is **TRUE**?

T or F The San Francisco 49ers football team is named after the gold miners.

T or F Most American gold seekers traveled to California by railroad.

Find the answers in this book.

A miner's pick

Contents

A gold pan

Panning for Gold

California's state motto, "Eureka," is a Greek word meaning, "I have found it!"

5 The Dark Side

6 End of the Gold Rush

An advertisement from the 1880s for Levi's jeans

James Marshall stands in front of Sutter's Mill.

CHAPTER 1

A Fantastic Discovery

On January 24, 1848, a carpenter named James Marshall made a discovery that changed U.S. history. He was building a sawmill for his business partner, John Sutter, beside a river in northern California's Sacramento Valley. Suddenly, something bright in the water caught his eye. Marshall bent down and picked up a piece of shiny metal. He had found gold!

← Marshall bit the metal he found as a test to find out if it was gold!

Some wagon trains traveled more than 2,000 miles (3,200 kilometers) to reach California.

In 1849, about 6,000 wagons traveled to California from the American Midwest.

Rush for Gold

Marshall and Sutter tried to keep their discovery a secret, but word got out and spread quickly. Soon the **gold rush** was on! Thousands of Americans and foreigners raced to California in search of gold. They came by ship and covered wagon. In the end, few of them struck it rich.

The Good and the Bad

Before Marshall's discovery, California was a **territory** of the United States. After the discovery of gold, it became the country's 31st state, in 1850. As gold seekers poured into California, new towns sprang up overnight. Money earned from gold was used to build factories and railroads. But the discovery of gold wasn't good for everyone. Native Americans, African Americans, and foreign **miners** were not treated fairly. And mining methods polluted the land.

During the gold rush, San Francisco, California, was a busy city.

Spanish explorers were among the first Europeans to visit the California coast.

CHAPTER 2

Before the Gold Rush

In the 1540s, the first Europeans in California were Spanish explorers. They were searching for a "city of gold" and for a river that was said to stretch from the Atlantic Ocean to the Pacific. Their searches were unsuccessful because neither the city nor the river actually existed. By 1775, Spain controlled a great deal of land in North America that included Mexico and present-day Texas and California.

Early Spanish explorers mistakenly believed that California was a gigantic island!

Lands of the West

By 1821, Mexico was no longer controlled by Spain, and it took over the rest of Spain's territories west of the Mississippi River. This made California part of Mexico.

The United States was also growing in size during this time. It became increasingly interested in Mexico's new territories. In 1835, and again in 1845, the U.S. government offered to buy California, but Mexico refused to sell the land.

This map of the United States in 1830 shows the territory controlled by Mexico.

Before the gold rush, most Californios lived on huge cattle ranches.

Californios round up thousands of cattle.

California Calling

In the 1830s, small numbers of people began moving from other parts of the United States to California. Most were traders, fur trappers or hunters, and adventurers. By the mid-1840s, California was home to about 1,000 Americans, several thousand Californios (Spanish-speaking settlers from Mexico), and more than 100,000 Native Americans.

Pioneers who were traveling west loaded their wagons with supplies at towns along the Missouri River.

Trouble for Mexico

By 1845, Mexico was losing much of the land it had controlled. Thousands of Americans known as **pioneers** were traveling west by wagon in search of better lives in California and the Pacific Northwest. Many of these pioneers believed that the United States had a right to expand its territories as far west as the Pacific Ocean. Over time, Americans living in Texas and California began pushing for freedom from Mexican rule.

California Victory

In 1835, Americans in Texas **revolted** against Mexico. Ten years later, Texas became America's 28th state. When a war broke out between the United States and Mexico in 1846, Americans in California also revolted. The war ended on February 2, 1848, with an American victory. Mexico gave the United States control of half of its territories, including California.

America's victory increased the size of the United States by about 525,000 square mi. (more than 1 million square km).

A miner uses a pan to collect gold from a stream.

CHAPTER 3

Gold Fever!

By August 1848, some 4,000 **prospectors** were digging, or mining, for gold in the hills above Sutter's property. Every man who could afford the price of a pick and a shovel had taken off for the goldfields. In San Francisco, the streets were empty. Soldiers had left their units, and sailors had abandoned their ships in port. Even San Francisco's newspapers had stopped printing.

Gold seekers destroyed Sutter's crops, stole his cattle, and tore down his buildings.

Heading South from Oregon

For six months, only people in California knew about the discovery of gold in their state. But in July 1848, the news was carried to Oregon by a ship's captain arriving there from San Francisco. Before long, Oregon newspapers were reporting that most Oregon men had gone to California to try their luck at gold mining. Oregon was suddenly faced with a shortage of lawyers, doctors, farmers, and even lawmakers!

Newspapers carried word of the discovery of gold in California to readers around the world.

EL DORADO
OF THE
UNITED STATES OF AMERICA.
THE DISCOVERY
OF
INEXHAUSTIBLE GOLD MINES
IN
CALIFORNIA.
TREMENDOUS EXCITEMENT AMONG THE AMERICANS.
The Extensive Preparations
TO
MIGRATE TO THE GOLD REGIONS,
&c., &c., &c.

The great discovery of gold, in dust, scales, and lumps of quicksilver, platina, cinnabar, &c., &c., on the shores of the Pacific, has thrown the American people into a state of the wildest excitement. The intelligence from California, that gold can be picked up in lumps, weighing six

Word Travels

By August, word of the gold strike reached the East Coast of the United States. A New York newspaper ran the headline: "GOLD! Gold from the American River!" Soon, newspapers throughout the country were writing stories about the discovery of gold. In December 1848, President James K. Polk officially announced that all the news reports were true. Now it was the world's turn to catch **gold fever**.

James K. Polk was president from 1845 to 1849.

In 1849 alone, 90,000 forty-niners went to California in search of gold.

Routes to California

The gold seekers who headed to California in 1849 were called **forty-niners**. About half of them took two different sea routes to San Francisco. The other half traveled to California overland on the Santa Fe, Oregon, and California trails. They made the long and difficult journey in covered wagons across the grasslands, deserts, and mountains of the American West.

Travel Dangers

Each of these routes was in some way dangerous. Many ships carrying forty-niners sank in rough waters. Gold seekers who traveled by wagon along the trails often feared attacks from Native Americans. But Indian attacks were rare. The biggest killer on the trails was a disease called cholera (KAHL-er-uh). A person could die from this severe illness within 24 hours of getting it. Cholera and other diseases killed thousands of forty-niners before they ever could reach California.

This pile of stones marks the grave of a pioneer who died while traveling west along the Oregon Trail.

The gold rush brought thousands of Americans and foreigners to mining camps.

CHAPTER 4

Life in the Land of Gold

Most forty-niners were unmarried men. They lived in dirty mining camps with names like Rough and Ready, Hangtown, Murderer's Gulch, and You Bet. Home was usually a tent or a wooden shack. Mining work was hard. Some forty-niners put in 16-hour days, six days a week. They dug dirt and moved big rocks. Throughout the long, hard days, their dreams of getting rich kept them going.

As soon as the gold was gone, many mining camps emptied out and became "ghost towns."

Miners often paid for food and supplies in "pinches," or small amounts, of gold dust. ➡️

Pay Days

At the beginning of the gold rush, some miners found as much as $300 worth of gold a day. Back then, most Americans earned only about $30 a

month. A miner might work for six months and return home with enough money in gold to live on for several years. Most prospectors found little gold.

A gold rush prospector with some of his tools

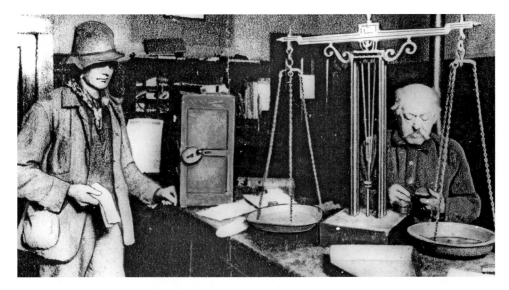

A prospector waits for a banker to weigh his gold dust. Prospectors were given money based on the gold's weight.

The Cost of Living

Most forty-niners made about $30 a day. However, a meal in San Francisco, Sacramento, or Stockton, three of the biggest gold rush towns, could cost more than $20. Boots sold for $20 a pair, coffee for $4 a pound, and eggs for 50 cents each. Before a miner knew it, his money was gone! Some miners also spent their money on bad habits, such as drinking and gambling.

Million-Dollar Ideas

The people who earned the most money at this time didn't work in the mines. Sam Brannan, a storeowner near Sutter's Mill, sold mining supplies to prospectors. He became the richest man in California. In 1850, Henry Wells, John Fargo, and others founded a speedy overland mail service between San Francisco and other U.S. cities. In 1852, Wells and Fargo started their own mail service.

More than 2,500 communities in 24 states were connected by Wells and Fargo's service.

Wells Fargo stagecoaches carried gold from California to the East Coast and returned with mail and packages.

Mr. Blue Jeans

In 1853, Levi Strauss, a tailor from Germany, journeyed to San Francisco and began making pants for gold miners. At first, he used canvas, a rough material. Later, he used a soft cotton cloth called denim. Miners loved his comfortable blue-colored pants, known as Levi's. In the 1870s, Strauss strengthened his pants by adding round copper pins that kept the pockets and seams from coming apart. Blue jeans were born!

Levi Strauss (above) was a poor tailor when he arrived in California. He became a millionaire by selling blue jeans to miners. These miners (right) are wearing Levi's jeans.

Women's Business

Women played an important role in the gold rush. By 1850, about 1,000 women from around the world were living in California. Some started their own businesses. Others earned extra money while their husbands searched for gold. Women ran small hotels, made home-cooked meals for miners, and did miners' sewing and laundry. Some women could make $50 to $100 a week washing miners' clothes.

Some women went to California to search for their own gold!

When they weren't working in the gold fields, some forty-niners spent their free time dancing and making music.

Rest and Relaxation

For entertainment, forty-niners enjoyed singing and making music. They also liked to bowl and play games, such as cards and pool. The most popular song of the gold rush period was "Oh! Susanna." One miner added his own words to this familiar tune while traveling to San Francisco by boat. His version grew so popular among miners that it became the unofficial theme song of the gold rush.

Panning for Gold

Miners had different ways of getting gold from the ground. The simplest method, called panning, was used along rivers. Miners would load dirt into a washing pan, which looked like a pie plate. Then they would hold the pan under water for a few minutes. The water would wash away lighter dirt, leaving heavier bits of gold behind. By 1852, most surface gold had disappeared, and panning was replaced by more costly mining methods.

Prospectors called the piles of dirt with bits of gold in it "pay dirt."

Mining camps could be rough and violent places.

CHAPTER 5

The Dark Side

In the early years of the gold rush, there were no laws or police in the goldfields. Robbery, "claim-jumping" (stealing another person's mining spot), and murder were common. Each mining camp set its own rules and punishments. However, these rules did not put an end to crime and violence.

A miner who broke his camp's rules could be kicked out or even hanged!

Many Native Americans worked as prospectors in the goldfields.

Tricks of the Trade

By 1848, about 150,000 Native Americans lived in California. After gold was discovered, thousands of them became prospectors. At first, these Native Americans did not realize how valuable gold was. Some miners tricked them by trading them worthless glass beads for gold. When tricks no longer worked, some miners formed gangs to drive Indians from the goldfields so they could steal their gold.

In 1848, more than half of all the gold prospectors were Native Americans.

Lost Land

Many Spanish-speaking Californios were also treated unfairly. By the end of 1849, about 90,000 people from outside of California had come to the state in search of gold. After living in California all of their lives, Californios suddenly discovered that they were considered outsiders. Then, as gold became harder to find, some American miners moved onto Californio-owned land and took it over.

Chinese Miners

Prospectors came to California from all over the world. Between 1848 and 1852, the number of Chinese people in San Francisco grew from almost zero to more than 20,000. Some American miners **discriminated** (diss-KRIM-uh-nate-id) against the hardworking Chinese. The Americans thought that California's gold should belong to Americans. They forced Chinese miners to pay special taxes and helped pass many anti-Chinese laws. Sometimes they even destroyed Chinese mining camps.

Gold Rush Timeline

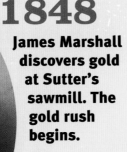

1848
James Marshall discovers gold at Sutter's sawmill. The gold rush begins.

1849
Thousands of forty-niners arrive in California from all over the world.

Limited Freedom

The gold rush began at a time when many African Americans were held as slaves in the United States. California did not allow its people to own slaves. But it did not stop slave owners from bringing enslaved people to California to mine gold. Sometimes these enslaved people escaped, hoping to find freedom. Many free African Americans from the East and North went to California to become prospectors.

1852
Most surface gold has been mined. Panning is replaced by more costly mining methods.

1850
California becomes the nation's 31st state.

The chemicals used in hydraulic mining poisoned the land and may still cause problems with the environment today.

CHAPTER 6

End of the Gold Rush

The gold rush lasted only a few years. By the early 1850s, most of the gold in streams and in fields had been taken. Finding buried gold became too difficult and expensive for prospectors to do on their own. Big mining companies moved in and took over. They used new mining methods, such as **hydraulic** mining, that blasted hillsides with powerful water hoses. This method helped companies wash away dirt from gold.

People in Rome, Spain, and England used hydraulic mining years before the gold rush.

The Golden Gate City

San Francisco was once a quiet village named Yerba Buena (YER-buh BWAY-nuh), after a kind of mint plant. During the short gold rush, it became America's largest western city. Between 1848 and 1850, the number of people living in San Francisco increased from 1,000 to 35,000. New homes and buildings were constructed, and new businesses were started to serve all of the people crowding into the city.

The Spanish settlement of Yerba Buena was renamed San Francisco in 1846.

This Japanese American farmer was among the people of many different cultures who made California home after the gold rush.

Lasting Effects

By the early 1860s, discoveries of gold and silver in other places led prospectors away from California. The gold rush had come to an end. But California was still a busy place that had become home to people from different **cultures**. Miners who stayed became farmers or business people. New cities were built that helped to complete America's expansion to the West Coast.

Visitors to Marshall's Gold Discovery State Historic Park learn how forty-niners mined for gold.

The Past Lives On

Today, many California towns still have names that were given to them during the gold rush. California's Highway 49 is named in honor of the forty-niners. The San Francisco 49ers football team was also named for the gold miners.

Throughout California, old mining towns have been rebuilt to look the way they did in 1849. Visitors can tour these towns and learn how the discovery of gold led to the growth of the United States. ★

True Statistics

Years the gold rush occurred: 1848 to 1853

Year California became a state: 1850

Early equipment used for finding gold: Pick, axe, shovel, pan

Length of the wagon route from Missouri to California: More than 2,000 mi. (3,200 km)

Biggest killer of people traveling west on the trails: Cholera

Value of a "pinch" of gold: About $16 (more than half of a man's monthly earnings in the 1840s)

Heaviest gold nugget ever found in California: 195 pounds (88 kilograms)

Value of all the gold mined from 1848 to 1853: $13 billion (in today's dollars)

Did you find the truth?

CALIFORNIA GOLD RUSH 1849

USA 3¢

T The San Francisco 49ers football team is named after the gold miners.

F Most American gold seekers traveled to California by railroad.

Resources

Books

Calabro, Marian. *The Perilous Journey of the Donner Party.* New York: Clarion Books, 1999.

Ferris, Julie. *California Gold Rush: A Guide to California in the 1850s.* New York: Kingfisher, 1999.

Landau, Elaine. *The Oregon Trail.* New York: Children's Press, 2006.

Manheimer, Ann S. *James Beckwourth: Legendary Mountain Man.* Minneapolis: Twenty-First Century Books, 2005.

Raum, Elizabeth. *The California Gold Rush: An Interactive History Adventure.* Mankato, MN: Capstone Press, 2008.

Saffer, Barbara. *The California Gold Rush.* Broomall, PA: Mason Crest Publishers, 2003.

Schanzer, Rosalyn. *Gold Fever!: Tales from the California Gold Rush.* Washington, DC: National Geographic Society, 1999.

Sonneborn, Liz. *Women of the American West.* New York: Franklin Watts, 2005.

Witteman, Barbara. *John Charles Frémont: Western Pathfinder.* Mankato, MN: Bridgestone Books, 2003.

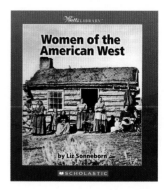

Organizations and Web Sites

California's Untold Stories: Gold Rush!

www.museumca.org/goldrush/

Find out about "gold fever" and see gold rush art!

**Huntington Library: Land of Gold Dreams:
California in the Gold Rush Decade 1848–1858**

www.huntington.org/Education/GoldRush/game/index.htm

Follow the stories of a pioneer girl and a Chinese immigrant boy during the California gold rush.

Wayback (U.S. History for Kids): Gold Rush

http://pbskids.org/wayback/goldrush/index.html

Take an imaginary journey with a forty-niner at this site.

Places to Visit

Gold Country Museum

1273 High Street
Gold Country Fairgrounds
Auburn, CA 95603
(530) 889-6500
www.placer.ca.gov/
Departments/Facility/
Museums/LocalMuseums/
goldcountry.aspx/
Tour a miner's cabin and a camp.

Wells Fargo History Museum

420 Montgomery Street
San Francisco, CA 94163
(415) 396-2619
www.wellsfargohistory.com/
museums/museums_sf.htm

See the stagecoach used by Wells Fargo in the 1860s and displays of real gold.

Important Words

cultures – the beliefs and ways of life of nations or peoples

discriminated (diss-KRIM-uh-nate-id) – judged or treated unfairly because of race, religion, gender, or other factors

forty-niners – nickname for the people who went to California in search of gold in 1849

gold fever – the desire to rush to California to find gold

gold rush – the mass movement of people to an area where gold has been recently discovered

hydraulic – operated by or powered by moving water or another liquid

miners – people who remove gold from a mine

pioneers – those who are the first to explore or live in a place

prospectors – people looking for valuable minerals and metals, especially gold

revolted – rose up or fought against a government or other authority

territory – an area or region of land that belongs to and is governed by a country

Index

Page numbers in **bold** indicate illustrations

About the Author

Mel Friedman is an award-winning journalist and children's book author. He has four graduate degrees from Columbia University, including one in East Asian studies. He also holds a bachelor's degree in history from Lafayette College. Friedman has written or cowritten more than two dozen children's books, both fiction and nonfiction. He and his wife and their daughter often rescue stray dogs.